Dealing with Feeling...
Happy

Isabel Thomas

Illustrated by Clare Elsom

Heinemann
LIBRARY
Chicago, Illinois

© 2013 Heinemann Library
an imprint of Capstone Global Library, LLC
Chicago, Illinois

Edited by Dan Nunn, Rebecca Rissman, and
 Catherine Veitch
Designed by Philippa Jenkins
Original illustrations © Clare Elsom
Illustrated by Clare Elsom
Production by Victoria Fitzgerald
Originated by Capstone Global Library, Ltd.
Printed in China

16 15 14 13 12
10 9 8 7 6 5 4 3 2 1

Library of Congress Cataloging-in-Publication Data
Thomas, Isabel, 1980-
 Happy / Isabel Thomas.
   p. cm.—(Dealing with feeling)
 Includes bibliographical references and index.
 ISBN 978-1-4329-7105-2 (hb)—ISBN 978-1-4329-7114-4 (pb) 1. Happiness in children—Juvenile literature. 2. Happiness—Juvenile literature. I. Title.
 BF723.H37T56 2013
 152.4'2—dc23   2012008277

Contents

Some words are shown in bold, **like this**. Find out what they mean in the glossary on page 23.

What Is Happiness?

happy

jealous

proud

sad

Happiness is a **feeling**. It is normal to have many kinds of feelings every day.

Some feelings are nice to have. Happiness is a nice feeling. You can help yourself to feel happy more often.

How Does It Feel to Be Happy?

When we are happy, we feel good about ourselves. Smiling or laughing shows other people how we feel.

Being happy makes us feel brave or **confident.** It helps us to do the things that we want to do.

What Makes People Happy?

Sometimes other people do things to make us happy, such as giving us a surprise present. We can also do things to make ourselves happy.

Many people feel happy if they do well at something. You can make yourself happy by working hard to do well in school and at home.

What Can I Do to Feel Happy?

Being around other people can make us feel happy. Talking and playing with friends and family is fun.

You can make new friends by smiling and saying, "Hello." Meet new people by playing sports or starting a new **hobby** outside school.

What If I Am Feeling Sad?

Everyone feels sad sometimes. Talking to someone can make you feel happier.

You can cheer yourself up by doing something you enjoy. Try reading a book or watching a funny movie.

How Can I Turn Sad Feelings into Happy Ones?

Feelings can change the way that people behave. What do you do when something makes you feel angry, sad, or **jealous**?

If you think happy thoughts it will help you to feel better. If you are cheerful and kind, people will do things to make you happy, too!

What Is the Quickest Way to Feel Happy?

Try frowning, then smiling. How do you feel inside? You can make yourself feel happier just by smiling!

Smiling makes other people feel friendly toward you, too. Who would you most like to be friends with in this picture?

What If I Have to Do Something I Don't Like Doing?

How do you feel when you are asked to clean up at school or at home? If people ask for your help, it means they think you will do a good job.

When you have finished, you will feel **proud**. The person you helped will be pleased. Helping other people can make YOU feel happy, too!

How Can I Make Other People Feel Happy?

Nobody feels happy all the time. Your friends and family might feel sad, angry, or worried sometimes.

They might want to talk about how they feel. You can help them to feel happier by listening and by being a good friend.

Make a Happiness Toolbox

Write down some tips to help you feel happy every day.

Set yourself a goal and work hard to do well at it.

Find a friend or family member to talk to.

Smile!

Read a book or watch a movie that you enjoy.

Go for a walk or a run outside.

If you feel sad, try doing something different.

Make others happy by helping them.

Learn a new **hobby** or sport.

Don't be afraid to ask for help. Everyone needs help sometimes.

Glossary

confident feeling that you can do something well

feeling something that happens inside our minds. It can affect our bodies and the way we behave.

hobby activity that you do for fun, in your own time

jealous feeling upset or grumpy that you do not have something that another person has

proud feeling pleased with yourself

Find Out More

Books

Bingham, Jane. *Happy (Everybody Feels).*
  New York: Crabtree, 2008.
Carlson, Nancy. *Smile a Lot!* Lerner, 2012
Medina, Sarah. *Happy (Feelings).*
  Chicago: Heinemann Library, 2007.

Internet sites

Facthound offers a safe, fun way to find Internet sites related to this book. All of the sites on Facthound have been researched by our staff.

Here's all you do:
Visit www.facthound.com
Type in this code: 9781432971052

Index